UNCOMMON SENSE
OR THE
21ST CENTURY FEDERALIST

UNCOMMON SENSE
OR THE
21ST CENTURY FEDERALIST

JH THOMPSON

ISBN-13: 9781543037197
ISBN-10: 1543037194

CONTENTS

ACKNOWLEDGMENTS
AND DEDICATION

I've dedicated this pamphlet to many people and a couple of institutions. I will try to keep this dedication shorter than the pamphlet. However, many individuals and organizations of which I and they have been a part of directly contributed to making me the person I am today and I'm eternally grateful for that.

To my country—the United States of America. My father had a "pickle wagon" saying whenever I asked for money. He would ask when I would pay him back (and if I was going to pay interest). He would ask me, "What if you got run over by the pickle wagon?" I rarely got the money. In reply to money inquiries, he would always answer, "I'm comfortable." We were middle class, never missed the necessaries, and rarely did without. We were comfortable. He never asked for much and had the requirements for life—a great wife, seven children, employment (usually), food on the table (always), shelter for the family, alcohol and Lucky Strikes, and good friends. He was happy, content, and comfortable.

My surviving brothers, Chris and Lee, two exemplary men, citizens, fathers, and friends. The best an older brother could have. And, if they were still alive, my parents, Harold and Elizabeth, and siblings Sheila, Richard, Robert, and Susan who would be there with encouragement, support, honesty, and love.

My country, by design or good fortune, has provided me and my family with an above comfortable life. Thanks to general fairness, opportunity, public education, family, and professional mentors, I've done, I believe, better than many, and I thank my country for that every day. As both parents would have wanted, I believe they would agree that I've done better than they did—in a good way.

The American Legion, and especially the Department of Utah, who has shown me over the past few years what my life would be like if I were selfish, dishonest, corrupt, of low character, and with no integrity and a total lack of morality and ethics and how my life would be so much different if these attributes and values were followed by more individuals, the county, state, corporations, and organizations I've dealt with or been a member of. They are truly the un-American Legion (and wonder why membership has fallen and hasn't been replenished even though we've had a pool of veterans for some sixteen years now).

My friends. Those people who have supported me, stood by me, and provided honest criticism and sincere congratulations when warranted. Mr. Rogers would like to live in my neighborhood.

My editors, Bill and Vicky, and their associates. Without my English teacher, my sister Sue, to assist me here, I'd be lost. For someone who has always loved English and literature, I've never been good at either, and without that assistance, regardless of how many people read this pamphlet, I'm appreciative and grateful for their patience, expertise, professionalism, and insight.

The US Marine Corps. The year 1967 probably wasn't the best year to fail college chemistry. Since I enlisted, all those men of high character, rightly guided patriotism, utmost integrity, unflinching professionalism, and the desire and will to always do what was right—my debt to them is enormous and can never be paid back. These men are heroes both on the battlefield and in an office. Just to name a few—Carroll, English, Himes, Berbaum, Dixon, Meadows, Griffin, Lofton (USA), Newbold, O'Brien, Brennen, Stackpole, Davis, Sullivan, Slough, Cook, Swisher, Fenlon, Nownes, Dishman, Zinni, Van Riper, and Jackson.

Most significantly, my family—Bonnie, a devoted wife, and loving children, Wendy, Kelly, and Zak. A man anywhere couldn't ask or have it better. Bonnie always had a soft, but accurate, critical eye and gave me encouragement in all my letters to the editor, articles in magazines, and commentaries; and whatever idea I had to pursue, she always said, "Go for it!"

And finally, my three grandchildren, Ricardo, Aaron, and Vivvi, who, are why I wanted to write this pamphlet. To them. I hope their lives and this country, it will be better for them than it was for their parents and grandparents.

PROLOGUE

*We have everything good government could
possibly want now but good government.*

—*Tu Fu, great seventh-century
Chinese poet and Taoist*

Let me be very clear—this pamphlet proposes to abolish the
Congress of the United States by an amendment article to the
US Constitution and to transfer the federal legislative function
over to the respective states.

Our federal system has made the United States great because
we had great people leading and great people serving as members
of our legislative branch. That degree of participation has been
sorely lacking over the past thirty years (since the early 1990s),
and without a catastrophic event or someone with some really

good charisma coming on the scene, I don't foresee that degree of participation returning during my lifetime. I want to leave my country in a better state than it is now to my grandchildren and to the rest of the country's grandchildren.

A major provision of this system allows us to change, adapt, and revise our Constitution, and it's generally understood that the reasons for doing so are to become a more perfect Union.

For those who are not politically or historically astute or may be lacking or forgetting some of their eighth-grade history, yes, the title of this pamphlet is a play on the wording of Thomas Paine's classic *Common Sense*—on why the United States should fight for and be separate from Great Britain—combined with *The Federalist*, by Madison, Hamilton, and Jay, in which the three wrote in support of adopting the Constitution.

The more I thought about how to convey and convince others that my proposal wasn't such a radical idea in the first place, the more I tried to start back at the beginning of our great country. There were, and are, many things that can earn a country the preface "great." Sometimes the word just covers a period of time, while sometimes it refers to the length of time the country has been around. This also applies to peoples, tribes, clans, cultures, and parties.

Let me also point out that this attempt started long before the recent political campaigns, and especially one by a certain public figure who used the word "great" in his campaign slogan. I was using the phrase for this proposal long before he started using it.

Phrases, sayings, and words only become great when those ideas and ideals are implemented. The Constitution is a great document, but like a dictionary or a holy book, it's only as good as the people who use it in the letter, spirit, and intent it was written for.

As this pamphlet gets ready to go into print, I wish to point to some recent thoughts during June 2017. I will mention this later on, but a book I just read was *A Fine Mess* by J. R. Reid (2017). It talks about our totally out-of-whack tax code, and next year (2018) is the cycle time for a complete revision as we do one, or have, every thirty-two or thirty-four years. I've become a believer in the concept of BBLR (broad base low rates) and the VAT (value-added tax). I encourage all to read the book and make up your own mind and consider the information about my ideas on how to balance the budget and how to make equal shares owed by each state.

Also of interest, this is the last month in office for Utah's own Jason Chaffetz (R-UT). There is a piling on of candidates for his seat, and, at least to me, it lends my proposal more credence for doing away with Congress. Among other issues, Utah is trying to decide who gets to decide how to replace him. The governor says it's up to him and his job; the legislature says they should have a say, but the governor will not call them into session. Rep. Chaffetz is known, among other things, for sleeping and living in his office, getting involved in DC politics, and investigating almost all Democrats who are in Congress.

He supposedly makes frequent trips back to Utah to be with his family and to find out what's going on in his constituency. Even though he lives in his office, he's not a resident of DC, nor can he vote there, but that doesn't seem to deter him from his small government philosophy of federal meddling in DC's Death with Dignity Act. Giving the gentleman from Utah the benefit of doubt, this proposal of mine will not be a problem for his replacement if we do away with Congress as all members would be able to live with their own constituencies.

I hope this proposal will enhance that goal of a more perfect Union for the United States of America for our next 228 years, just as it has done for the past 228 years—if we can last that long.

And for the support of this Pamphlet, with a firm reliance on the protection given me of Divine Providence and the first article of amendment to the US Constitution, I pledge the rest of my Life, my Fortune, and my sacred Honor. DONE in Ogden, Utah this 4th Day of July in the Year of Our Lord two thousand and Seventeen and of the Independence of the United States of America the two hundred and forty-second.

Article I

WHY?

*To preserve the memories and incidents
of the 2 World Wars and the other great
hostilities fought to uphold democracy.*

—UNITED STATES CODE (A),
TITLE 36, CHAPTER 21702

L et me be clear on why I am writing this pamphlet. I propose to abolish the Congress of the United States of America. This is an idea that occurred to me years ago, under the administration of George W. Bush, because of my disagreement and opposition to the wars on terrorism—to some degree in Afghanistan but mainly (and most seriously) the invasion of Iraq.

When I first put my proposal into writing as a commentary in a local newspaper, my family, friends, and other people asked me if I was serious. In part as a result of my frustration with President Bush, but mostly with the Congress and its displayed lack of courage (and even less leadership), I became more and more serious and supportive of the idea.

Before 1900, the US sent troops abroad 103 times, usually to protect US business interests.

—RICK JONES, VIEWPOINTS, STANDARD-EXAMINER, DECEMBER 16, 2016

I am a veteran of the US Marine Corps. Because of my service, I am eligible to join various veterans' organizations. During all my years of service—including active, reserve, inactive reserve, inactive, and retired—I've never questioned the what or why in the use of the US Armed Forces. I accepted that condition when I decided to stay involved and wear the uniform. The reason that would be important to me would be the reason my commander or supervisor provided, if and when he or she provided it.

The quote at the beginning of this article is from the act of Congress that created the American Legion by granting a national charter in 1919, with subsequent minor revisions since. The reason I've mentioned this quote is because I've found no justification in any of these wars that I believed met the "uphold democracy" portion of the statement. I will also assume that the wording is similar (if not the same) for the other veterans' organizations chartered by Congress. It is clear to me that the reasons our armed forces were committed to those wars do not match up with the criteria for joining a veterans' organization. My point is that these reasons, and definitions, have both come from the same Congress. This is not a good thing.

I've never questioned the taking or retaking of the appropriate-level oath, as is customary for a Marine upon enlistment, reenlistment, commissioning, and promotion. I always kept the oath in the forefront of my thoughts wherever I performed my duties, especially on significant national observance days such as the Fourth of July, Presidents' Day, Constitution Day (September 17), Veterans Day, and Memorial Day. It was also humbling to me as a Marine to retake the oath every four to six years upon promotion to a higher grade.

> *The single most important thing we*
> *want to achieve is for President Obama*
> *to be a one-term president.*
>
> *—SEN. MITCH MCCONNELL,*
> *(R-KY), OCTOBER 23, 2010*

Marines are not required to retake the oath when they are promoted. By tradition, however, Marines often retake the oath to emphasize their support and defense of the Constitution upon promotion. The oath is required, and it is based on Article VI of the Constitution.

The oath is a modification, by code, of the same oath required to be taken by the president (Article II, Section 1). This is where the wording "preserve, protect, and defend the Constitution of the United States" comes from. It is the same in all the oaths; portions of the rest of the oath are slightly modified depending on if you're joining the enlisted ranks or becoming a mayor, an associate justice of a supreme court (state or federal), or a member of Congress. Article VI is where the word "support" comes from.

During the fall of 2001, most of my friends and coworkers believed in and supported the first war; later on, during 2002 and 2003, they did the same for the second war. I disagreed with them. What democracy (or "-ies") were we fighting to uphold in Afghanistan or Iraq?

I know no way of judging the
future but by the past.

—*Patrick Henry*

I told them that I didn't care what people said on talk radio or on local and national TV, and I especially didn't care what Utah's elected members of Congress said. They were wrong: Saddam Hussein had no weapons of mass destruction. Furthermore, it was my belief that we couldn't—and shouldn't—afford these wars. Nor would we have the intelligence or political fortitude or courage to pay for the wars. And those people (and I'm purposely not using the word "leaders" here) who would or did decide to go to war were disconnected and unfamiliar with those in the armed forces who would actively be fighting and suffering and sacrificing and dying in the wars. It has happened numerous times before, and I was sure it was going to happen again during this reiteration of our history.

Now, in light of President Clinton's success in balancing the budget, starting to pay down the national debt, and turning over to President Bush a surplus amount, we were starting first one, and then a second, war. I believe firmly, and always have, that we as a country should have a balanced budget.

There went the budget and debt again. As of this writing (June 2017), our national debt is a disgraceful $20,000,000,000,000— that's $20 trillion.

> *A warrior fights for his brothers, not for*
> *glory or his life, not to abandon them,*
> *not to Prove unworthy of them.*

> —DIENEKES, GATES OF FIRE

Yes, I'm a firm believer in a balanced budget and in paying for the goods, products, and services you've contracted for. It is my belief that these wars—in addition to the reasons and ways in which they were fought—were a colossal waste of money.

Back to the Constitution. Many nonveterans believe that members of the armed forces died for the Constitution, the flag, and the country during these wars. I, and many veterans I know, disagree with this statement. We believe that these people sacrificed their lives because of a sense of loyalty, comradeship, professionalism, and love. Mom, flag, and apple pie are much further down the list.

That being said, for whatever reasons men and women join the armed forces, they are required to take that oath. How many of them know what the oath means? Have they ever read the Constitution? I would venture to guess that very few of them have.

Voter turnout in 2014 was dismal. In Utah, local turnout was about 28 percent, while statewide it was 37 percent; nationally it was 46 percent. This is our democracy! Voting is a right that countless veterans have enlisted, fought, become disabled, and died to secure for all of us. Over the course of the past fifteen to twenty years, the Congress has become, and stayed, dysfunctional. The most recent Congress suffered a 14 percent approval rating. A rating this high tells me that Congress took part in the survey. For years, no budget was passed. The deficit and debt grew out of control. Basic laws failed to be passed. Everything seemed to become a partisan dog fight, most of the time ending up in a blockage of procedures. At the very worst, things simply did not get done.

Members of Congress have their political ideologies when it comes to the issues, but they depend far too greatly on political action committees (PACs), lobbyists, special interests, and their donors to actually tell them how policy, laws, and legislation should be written or revised.

Regardless of why people joined the armed forces, at least they performed their duties in a professional, competent, and successful manner. The same can't be said for members of Congress. Is it asking too much for members of Congress to honor their oath just as members of the armed forces are bound to honor theirs?

It was this environment that pushed me to put my thoughts on paper. I originally intended to write a novel but decided instead that I was more serious about this than a novel would lend itself to be. I also felt that, due to my writing skills, I would have a significantly better chance at completing a pamphlet than a novel. Hence this attempt.

People would ask me how, under this system, the country would work without Congress. This pamphlet will not try to convince you that I have all the answers to that question—no more than the Founding Fathers had when they came up with the approved, final consensus of the first Constitution and how Congress, the executive branch, or the courts would function. But I do hope this proposal will provide a workable outline to accomplish that goal, because we surely need a better system than what we have now.

> *Sen. McConnell has said he won't hold a*
> *vote on a nominee until after the election.*
> *Even then, he says, he won't guarantee it.*

> —*TIME, AUGUST 29, 2016*

In short, my proposal would amend the Constitution by turning over the national/federal legislative function to the states. Under our federal system, we already have many of these mechanics in place. I'm not proposing to do away with federal laws or functions nor, especially, the president. By using the Constitution and offering some rewording in order to amend the Constitution, I hope to put forth a realistic, serious, and better form and system of government.

Some notes regarding the appendices. Appendix A is a serious but maybe a layman's attempt at revising the US Constitution for a few reasons. The first was to delete all references to Congress and replace that word (Congress) with Congregation, which, for now, is what I would be calling the meeting or coordinating together of the state legislatures in replacing Congress as the maker of federal laws. I've also updated some grammar and wording to more modern usage. The second reason was to combine all the amendments into the basic document where they changed, modified, or revised some constitutional process or procedure. This to me was common sense and logical in putting all related issues together in the same article/section. Because the first ten amendments were added and did not change anything in the original document, I've left those ten amendments (the Bill of Rights) separate as appendix B.

Appendix C contains limited information and stats on the fifty states and Washington, DC. I've used this information to compare the states in my quest to come up with a better way to try and make the states more equal and equable where possible in light of doing away with Congress and trying to ensure, to whatever degree possible, that all states are treated fairly both in making federal laws and in the enforcement of federal laws. Appendix D is old information, based on certain criteria, used in an effort based on taxation when discussing a state's influence on federal laws, using a comparison between what citizens of a state pay in federal taxes compared with what those citizens (directly or indirectly) get back from the federal government in taxes. I believe there should be a clear difference between when taxes pay for people employed by the federal government and government products and services and when taxes are allocated back to states in grants, subsidies, contracts, and so on.

Why shouldn't this proposal be taken seriously? My authorities are the Declaration [of Independence] and the Constitution. The Declaration states that "whenever any form of Government becomes destructive of these ends" (those ends being unalienable rights), it is the "Right of the People to alter or to abolish it." Congress now meets that definition of a form of government needing to be altered or abolished. These statements were true in June–July 1776 and are even more true today.

I consider myself, at best, to be a mediocre writer. Since my English teacher, my sister Sue, isn't alive to help me, I accept full responsibility for what I've now written. Sir Harold Evans recently wrote *Do I Make Myself Clear?* and was interviewed by Edward Felsenthal in *Time* for 10 Questions. Given the interview, I hope I didn't fail and at least came close to putting words down that don't deceive and have expanded, explained, and given some examples and that my writing could be categorized as at least better than a "vomit draft" (credit to Tina Brown).

> *Those who cannot remember the past*
> *are condemned to repeat it.*
>
> —GEORGE SANTAYANA

Article V of the Constitution authorizes amendments, either (1) from the Congress or (2) from application of state legislatures (both by two-thirds majority) in calling for a convention and then receiving a three-quarter approval vote by the states.

We are in the 21sr century. The modes of communications and video conferencing we have—and the various ways we can process, send, and receive data, information, studies, reports, surveys, and statistics—are beyond anything the Founding Fathers dreamed of, thought of, or contemplated. But they knew they didn't know all that might happen, which is why they allowed for the Constitution to be amended in the first place. Are "We the People" still content to give our permission and consent to those who govern us? I'm not. Are those procedures that were set forth in the 18th century really still the best way to go for the United States in the 21st century?

> *Poll: Three-quarters of Americans*
> *say they lack influence in D.C.*

> —*SALT LAKE TRIBUNE/THE AP, JULY 16, 2017*

Let's see.

Article II

DYSFUNCTIONAL CONGRESS

There is only one way to avoid criticism;
do nothing, say nothing, be nothing.

—*ARISTOTLE*

This proposal of mine isn't an attempt to convince you with facts, figures, statistics, examples, or comparisons. I've purposely not included footnotes and references. I've used that thing between my ears known as a "brain-housing group" and have recalled a few recent newspaper reports of incidents that I believe support my proposal. If you think the system works well and we're now the best we can be, then no amount of factual information is going to convince you otherwise.

When people first heard of this proposal, every one of them was taken aback and said that there was no way our country could function without a Congress. But once I mentioned turning it over to the states, some of them at least became interested; as we had the time and I was able to explain more to them, at least they became a little more receptive to the idea. I will state, however, that I never convinced anyone.

I've become more convinced of my own idea over the last thirteen months for three reasons: (1) the annual meeting for forty-five days of the Utah legislature; (2) this mess of a system called the presidential party nominating process; and (3) the death of Antonin Scalia and the refusal of the Republicans in the Senate to speak with, much less hold hearings on, the president's choosen successor. Is this the best we can do?

I did do some research other than what's available in the newspapers, and I found many books on Congress. Basically, there's an abyss between what's written in the Constitution and what a member of Congress believes a member's sworn duty and responsibility should be.

Some of the books I like include *Facts about the Congress*, by S. G. Christianson (1996); *Do Not Ask What Good We Do*, by Robert Draper (2012); *So Damn Much Money*, by Robert G. Kaiser (2013); and *How Congress Works and Why You Should Care*, by Lee H. Hamilton (2004).

I'll list quotes below from the books that I liked and deem pretty relevant to my proposal. For those who are interested, plenty of books—and many more recent than these—are available in the local library and online.

*Do not ask what good we do: That is not
a fair question, in these days of faction.*

—REP. FISHER AMES, FEDERALIST
MA, MAY 30, 1796

Draper's book is about the dysfunctional 112th Congress, which was elected in 2010 (along with a Republican majority) but had an overall approval rating of only 9 percent. Congress more than once brought the nation to the brink of government shutdown or economic default. The book is about how Americans lost faith in their democratic institutions.

I really like Hamilton's writings. He represented (in a very good way) Indiana's Ninth District from 1965 to 1999. His very informative *How Congress Works and Why You Should Care* includes many letters to the editors that have been printed in local newspapers over the years. Here are a few of the ideas he includes in the book.

* Congress is the dominant branch of government.
* Power drifts to the president when Congress doesn't live up to its responsibilities.
* The first role of Congress is to act as a check on the power of the president (i.e., to maintain freedom). Hamilton stated this after hearing a radio-show commentator say, "We'd be a lot better off if we just did away with Congress."
* He points out that the many differences within the representatives in Congress is a reflection of the country's many differences.

* He includes this quote from Sen. Robert Wagner: "If a government or a people is to progress, its goal must ever be a little beyond its reach."
* If members of Congress can't get things done due to gridlock, they should be reviewing old laws with that goal in mind.
* In a *Federalist* paper, Madison wrote that a member of Congress needed to understand just three things: commerce, taxation, and the militia.
* Constituents represent a double-edge responsibility: Should members of Congress serve their constituents or the country?
* Congress should first favor the national interest, but most all now openly lean toward local interests.
* FDR judged all legislation by the simple question, "How does it affect ordinary people?"
* Our goal for government should be that government should much more often than not be part of the solution rather than part of the problem.
* Election winners should work for everyone.
* Common efforts for the common good are for the good of the country.
* Congress is too busy to look too far ahead.
* Washington, DC, has twenty-five thousand lobbyists (see previous statement),
* Congressional oversight is a neglected but important responsibility of both the legislative and executive branches.

* Democracy is the process, not the product. The process helps ensure transparency, openness, accessibility, and accountability. Four important parts of the process are (1) voting, (2) communicating with representatives, (3) being informed, and (4) being involved in your community.
* Citizen participation is the right and responsibility to be involved in one's governance.
* A two-way conversation should take place between representatives and citizens, and both sides should educate the other side.

Overall, *How Congress Works* is complimentary much of the time. The first book, *Facts about the Congress*, is just a compilation of major bills that became law, who ran the Congress, and an overview of each two-year Congressional session. The other two books, *Do Not Ask What Good We Do* and *So Damn Much Money*, deal with the overall corrupting influence of money in politics, including dirty politics, how deals are made, and the disproportionate weight that PACs, lobbyists, special interests, and other people have in proposing, running through, and getting their bills passed into law. Many times they are able to do so without a window crack of sunshine being allowed during the process.

Is this what we want? Do these things meet the criteria of being a "great" democratic country? Is this a functional or dysfunctional institution? Regardless of what type of government you believe we have—democracy, republic, representative democracy, no government, and the like—you have to agree that it is not working the way it should.

Mind you, I usually agree with the philosophy that sometimes not all problems have to be solved. But I also believe that for several decades now, the Congress has not performed in anywhere near an exemplary manner by fixing, resolving, or solving some of the major issues that it should have addressed and solved. We have to get back to always keeping in mind why the word "United" is in the name of our country.

This is purely my opinion, but a few of those problems include the national debt; the immigration situation; our foreign-policy positions; the income-tax structure; the inequality between our low-, middle-, and high-income earners; and our education systems.

In Utah, since it's a very deep "red" state, we also have the federal-overreach discussion, the federal-lands problem, and the recently passed resolution that would repeal the Seventeenth Amendment and return to having states' legislatures elect senators once again. (My proposal here makes this issue moot as well as takes the process one step further.)

> *Trump is a product of our political system's*
> *failure to adapt to demographic change, economic*
> *disruption and a reorganizing world.*
>
> —*Eugene Robinson, Washington*
> *Post, February 28, 2016*

We all want to believe our position is right. We can have differences of opinion on how something should be done and why something should be done. Many people feel that the running of a government should be akin to running a business. I disagree, mainly because the objectives are totally different—it's profit and growth versus safety and service.

My first comment to my friends when they bring this up to me—especially since 2012, with Mitt Romney's business background, and now of course with Donald Trump and his business credentials for seeking the presidency—is, "Do you really believe that anyone could run a government like a business?"

They generally answer no, and they admit that it's just a nice political slogan. The rules are completely different, as are the structures of both operations. Having said this, based on what Congress should do and what it actually spends its time on, if Congress were a business and you were the CEO, would you not fire every one of its members?

What does Congress cost now? On a quick check, I came up with the following figures: one study (from 2013) found that it costs around $804 million per year, while another study came up with a $30,000-per-day amount. This is an interesting question, and the figures here are guesstimates.

Let's start with just the members. If we use a rounded annual salary of $150,000 and the fact that Congress has 535 members, then that's easily over $80 million per year in salary. This of course does not include other benefits, such as cost-of-living expenditures, health care, retirement, or travel. Nor does it cover the upkeep and operation of the Capitol. Also, not included are the costs of reports, research, staff (and all related personnel costs), utilities, vehicles, and numerous other charges related to keeping those buildings running.

Yes, this is all a drop in the financial bucket. But if you run a business or have any business experience, then you know the primary costs of such businesses go to people. If you'd hired someone who didn't do his or her job and didn't perform to a minimum standard or met basic employment standards, would you still keep paying that person?

Now, how big are these staffs? Using the analogy of any business or private enterprise, the largest costs to run a business are personnel costs, so we can't forget the staffs. These staffs average 17 personnel per representative and 40 per senator. At an average of around $50,000 per person and for, say, 17 people for each of the 535 members, this salary, without those other benefits, runs to over $727 million per year. I won't make a guess about utilities and telecommunications costs for the Capitol or the other seven to nine buildings that Congress and staff regularly use.

After 221 years, the earlier quote by Representative Ames to a fellow representative is just as true then as it would be today.

We are getting nothing done.

—*SENATOR JOHN MCCAIN, FLOOR OF THE US SENATE, JULY 25, 2017*

Article III

REPRESENTATION

*All legislature Powers herein granted
shall be vested in a Congress.*

—*US Constitution, Article I, Section 1*

To represent—what does this mean?

No doubt many things to different people. Are we a democracy or a representative democracy or a republic? I'll go with representative democracy, as we surely are not a democracy, because everyone can't vote (or doesn't vote), and certainly, if based on the way we elect a president, we certainly are not a democracy.

I also would not say that we are a republic, based on the definition that this is where a government is completely elected. When we have (as we do) people who elect people to elect people, as we do for president, or when we have state legislatures elect the senators, that is not even representative government. So by default, we are a representative democracy.

Should we be, as we most certainly could be, a purer democracy at the state and national level? I believe we could be based on technology, but considering the dismal participation rate, I'm not sure this is a good idea, at least for now.

Do representatives—I'm talking about the House of Representatives here, but my philosophy pertains to this position at all levels—just represent the people who voted for them? Do they represent all who voted? What about people who just work in the district but don't live there? What about anyone who visits the district? What about minors—those who can't yet vote? What about those who don't even register to vote?

I'm of the opinion that representatives, rather than having a narrow viewpoint, should represent all those people, interests, areas, and activities they might affect by the legislation their legislative bodies pass.

The answer or reason I believe is obvious to me—because, as stated, actions of representatives do affect more than just those in their district or electorate. I'd bet that usually their actions affect many times more than those just in their district, especially, many times over, those who just voted for that representative.

One reason I believe that many, if not most, take the much narrower view is that it's easier and more convenient to do so. Why deal with ten times more issues and special interests than necessary? Except for political contributions, why put up with more input than you have to? Reelection becomes the paramount and overriding factor in all actions.

Any legislator should always, first and foremost, have the interest of the largest political entity at heart. Hence, a representative should consider first what's best for the United States. A state legislator should act first for the benefit of the state as a whole. That responsibility is now the sole prerogative or responsibility of, respectively, the president or the governor. Or, I should add, the party, the sole objective of which is to get elected and gain power.

Back to my veteran's status and oath to support and defend our Constitution against all enemies, foreign and domestic. Paul S. Gardiner (LTC, US Army [Ret.]) wrote in August 2016 about the Convention of States (COS) Project. He leads a group of concerned veterans in appealing to state legislatures to pass resolutions to require Congress to call for a Constitutional Convention with the goal of restoring the balance of power between the federal and states governments. He believes action has to be taken now and legislators will listen to veterans. Some eight state legislatures have passed resolutions calling for a Constitutional Convention. The project's goal is to get the constitutionally required thirty-four states' legislatures to pass resolutions for this purpose.

Many people feel this type of constitutional amendment process (rather than the congressional method) is too open-ended, because it allows any proposed amendment to be considered. You might remember that this is what happened at our first Constitutional Convention, when the delegates were supposed to meet just to revamp the Articles of Confederation.

> *Last year some 12,000 lobbyists spent $3.24B*
> *on trying to influence the federal government,*
> *according to the Center for Responsive Politics.*

—*LEE HAMILTON, LETTER TO THE EDITOR,*
STANDARD-EXAMINER, DECEMBER 5, 2014

The COS Project, however, wants to limit the convention to three purposes: (1) impose fiscal restraints on the federal government, (2) limit the jurisdiction/power of the federal judiciary, and (3) limit the terms of office for its officials including members of the federal judiciary.

I don't agree, but I can sympathize with the thought, that veterans have earned a greater right here than the average citizen (just based on the action of having taken a constitutional oath at least once), and I do not necessarily agree with the three areas, especially because the exact wording has not yet been determined the last time I checked.

Here's another story about what passes for our representation. In April 2016, *60 Minutes* profiled Rep. David Jolly (R-FL). The program noted that House business was scheduled around fundraising. As a Republican, Jolly had a goal of raising some $18,000 a day; this state of affairs was opened up by the *Citizens United* decision. Call centers were set up by the Republican National Committee close to the Capitol, and members of Congress were encouraged to spend four hours calling and two hours on the House floor. The money that was raised was partially for Jolly, but most went to a National Republican Congressional Committee for funding its war chest.

Talk about money being the grease (and sleaze) of politics.

Every citizen should be his or her own representative. The Founding Fathers (thinking as 18th century gentlemen) wanted the average citizen at the time to be active, aware, involved, and a participant in our American democracy. This was the driving purpose of our public-education system. We need to get them both back.

Article IV

THE STATES

*A woman made a request of Hadrian
[Roman emperor, 117–138]. He replied "I
haven't got the time." She replied, "Well, stop
being emperor." He gave her a hearing.*

HADRIAN, AND THE TRIUMPH OF ROME
BY ANTHONY EVERITT *(2009)*

*The powers delegated by the proposed
Constitution to the federal government are few
and defined. Those which are to remain in the
state governments are numerous and infinite.*

—FEDERALIST *45*

I will limit this pamphlet to the fifty states and Washington, DC. I acknowledge Washington, DC, Puerto Rico, and the South Pacific territories with their respective representation in the Congress. They should be included somehow, but I'm not going to address their participation here other than DC, because DC is mentioned in the Constitution.

I'll limit state statistics and demographics to only certain areas. These, for the discussion, will be population, square miles, electoral votes, and the number of members in the state legislature. Granted, many other factors can be included (taxes paid to the federal government, federal benefits received, average/median income, number of federal jobs, and the like), but for ease and simplicity of discussion, we'll use only those listed. These are listed only as a starting point in order to set forth some type of method in which rights and benefits are universal; the granting of federal favors should be equal if not proportional or prorated. This also pertains to the representation discussion. See appendix C, "The Fifty States and Washington, DC, by Groupings."

This is not going to be a history lesson. Interested readers can do their own research. Suffice it to say that the Founding Fathers went through a few machinations in determining how to set up Congress.

Our current system, with the House and Senate, was compromised and implemented somewhere between the Virginia (big state) plan and the New Jersey (small state) plan. Of course the big compromise was the electing of the executive.

In case you never knew this (or you have forgotten), let me remind you that in this representative democracy of ours, our president only needs 270 votes to be elected. Regardless of how many of our national population of some 320 million people vote, only 270 count as determined by state legislatures, which is a majority of the 539 electoral votes available.

Another interesting piece of constitutional information here is that we could even elect a president with only eighteen votes. How? Glad you asked. The Constitution states that if no one gets a majority, then the race is thrown to the House. If a candidate who is elected dies before taking the oath of office, then the race is also thrown to the House. The House, voting by state, only requires a two-thirds majority or quorum to decide this issue. Hence, if thirty-four states are present (at the minimum), and a majority is only required to elect a president, then a candidate will only need eighteen votes to be elected president.

> *Washington is becoming less effective at*
> *addressing many of our nation's problems*
> *and less consequential in bolstering the cities*
> *and regions that drive the economy.*
>
> —BRUCE KATZ, WASHINGTON
> POST, NOVEMBER 28, 2014

Yes, I support changing the way we elect our president to be by popular vote, but I leave that matter for another pamphlet.

I guess no one ever discussed the idea of keeping all states within a given population range, with due consideration for limited geographical considerations. This might have avoided a few economic and political disagreements down the road, but that's now ancient history.

Sen. Lee (R-UT) says Flint has no need for federal
assistance, argues Michigan has enough money.

—*SALT LAKE TRIBUNE, MARCH 2016*

If we turn over our national legislative function to the states, how would we determine who's in charge? Who would propose legislation? Who would run it through the states and how? What would be the voting minimum to pass laws? Should that minimum vary by the type of law that's being passed?

A system must or should be in place to avoid the big-state–small-state confrontation. The current system of using seniority clearly hasn't worked very well, and my basic objection is that it isn't fair. Why is it that when someone is elected numerous times from a small district, or a small state, such reelection makes that person the most experienced or knowledgeable member, at the expense of a newly elected member of Congress? My personal opinion has always been that those newly elected members should be the ones who are in charge, since they were elected with the most knowledge or information of what people were thinking of—politically, economically, socially, and culturally—during the most recent election. This is especially true if he or she has just beat an incumbent.

To find real solutions, just look to the real
innovators—states, our laboratories of democracy.
My initiative will showcase those breakthroughs.

—*NATIONAL GOVERNORS ASSOCIATION*
(NGA) CHAIR GARY HERBERT,
GOVERNOR OF UTAH, JULY 2015

I've always thought that the newest members should be in charge and chairing committees, because they are the ones who were most recently elected, they are the closest to new ideas and old frustrations, and they have the most enthusiasm and desire for change and new ways of doing things. To a degree, this includes incumbents, but because majority of the incumbents are easily reelected (especially in the House), this philosophy of mine is now a little diluted, but I still support new members. Take Senator Hatch and former representative Hansen: Bozo the Chimp could cast a Republican vote, so what's the difference?

This was especially true years ago when you had an all-powerful party boss (or bosses) but now a little diluted with somewhat powerful factions within a party (i.e., the Tea Party members). But it is also true that funding by the national party apparatus still holds sway. Cross the majority leader, don't get out of state funding, lose your seat. Politics!

> *Taking the GOP "from being an opposition party to being a proposition party."*
>
> —*Speaker Paul Ryan (R-WI),*
> *Time, December 28, 2016*

Older, more senior members probably have a better and deeper knowledge of how the parliamentarian system and rules of each house works, but they may not have the best feel for what recent voters feel or think about current issues. They maintain the old "bring home the bacon" philosophy, which is the "don't rock the boat, don't make waves, and don't tip over the apple cart" approach.

These are just other ways of saying "keep the status quo." Since when has the United States ever been content with, much less successful at, keeping the status quo?

Article V

CHANGING THE PROCESS

Whatever you have anything to do with,
your first thought should be to improve it.

—*E. H. HARRIMAN TO HIS YOUNG*
SON, WILLIAM AVERELL

I will reiterate that abolishing Congress cannot, or should not, be done until our budget, deficit, debt, fiscal, and monetary house is put in order. How often do you remember Congress passing (or not passing) legislation after members checked with each state to see what the different states' positions were, either in support of or in opposition to the particular legislation?

Under our federal system, it is only fair, before making a federal law, that each state should know what it will be charged for the services, products, benefits, or programs that will be implemented because of that law. The states currently are not usually assessed or tasked; the citizens or populations are.

Is this right? No doubt this is correct as it's what's in place now, but is it right, or can a better process be implemented? Two examples are federal entitlements and our wars on terrorism. I believe our mind-set would be completely changed if for both of these we somehow assessed for each state what their share of the cost would be to pay for them. Would the states agree to this or not?

This process can be divided or separated out in many ways, some of which include by population. Another can be on some type of prorated basis of income. Still another could be by the overall wealth (however that is determined) of the state. It could be by entry into the Union, alphabetically by state, or by the last name of the governor. Finally, it could be by taxes and/or income of each state (individual or corporate, or both).

> *House GOP Benghazi investigation finds*
> *no wrongdoing by Clinton. This after*
> *two years and $7M tax payer dollars.*

> —SALT LAKE TRIBUNE, APRIL 2016

Life is not fair, nor equal, nor equitable. But government should at least strive for that goal. What I mean here is that the federal government must be uniform in dealing with the states. This is mainly seen through fiscal eyes but also can be seen in other areas. For instance, years ago the federal government wanted to store nuclear waste outside of the populous states that benefited from the nuclear fuel. Was it fair to attempt to store that waste in less populated states? Not to me.

Numerous studies have been done on government spending. After local city council meetings in which the presentation includes the idea that the cost of a program or grant will be borne (in whole or part) by federal dollars, I always like to point out that these are still real dollars. Everyone always thinks this is free money, and I can't think of one program that was not approved by the city council. I simply mention that this is still *your* money, because where do you think these federal dollars are coming from? The good citizens of Ogden are still paying for these programs and for many other programs in many other states and in many other cities. Would it be cheaper and more efficient if that grant money didn't get sent to DC but was instead collected locally? I prefer the analogy of comparing owners and renters. Using your own money (i.e., local taxes) causes you to monitor and maintain a longer-term interest in what that money will be spent on.

It's no secret that Congress, since the beginning of time (at least US Constitution time), has prided itself on how much "pork" it brings home, either directly or indirectly. I disagree with this system but acknowledge that it's in fact our current political life. I just believe, or at least hope, that there's got to be a better, fairer, and more equal and equitable way to do this.

How?

Let's start the conversation with one of two ways, depending on whether the issue at hand is fiscal or manpower related. If it's a fiscal issue, then the state is given its cost up front, based on its prorated share of the program's expense. This is money that's due up front before the program will get off the ground. If the issue is manpower—say, armed forces recruiting—then the number of enlistments and officers required to be commissioned is determined up front. This would be especially true if we're talking about getting into, or are already in, a war.

Of course we could do everything by dividing all requirements by fifty-one, but that's not going to happen. The point is—as I think this whole Union thing was set up in the first place—all states were to expect equal and fair treatment in federal issues, and all states were to benefit and sacrifice equally regarding costs and bad times.

Federal dollars are paid by corporate, income, and tariff taxes. The federal government, in all its generosity, gives back to the states much of this money. "Gives" might be the wrong word, but let's use it. This money comes back in the form of various programs, grants, wages, and salaries: things such as defense spending, NASA, Medicaid, Medicare, drug benefits, social security, retirement, disability, and farm subsidies.

I'm not advocating which programs are to be used. I'm pointing out that some process or procedures could be set up to ensure, if not guarantee, that each state is treated fairly, both in contributing and receiving the results of these taxes and benefits.

There are many websites that break down federal dollars paid in versus federal dollars paid back to states. These can be by each state or more likely for each tax payer in the state. What I've never been able to determine is what makes up the dollar figures. For instance, is it just grants and loans, tax refunds, or federal jobs or retirement or what? I determined it doesn't matter. Whatever basis is used and applied to all states is what counts and if we insist on keeping this system of taking and giving, we have to have as our goal that it becomes one dollar for one dollar.

TaxFoundation.org had stats from 2011 (see appendix D). There were seventeen states that received less than a dollar back for each dollar paid, with Rhode Island breaking even at one dollar paid to and one dollar returned from the federal government. If you took the next twenty-five states, you would average out that one dollar paid for those first seventeen states. This means that seven states got back over a dollar more than they paid in. Is this fair? Does anyone not realize now, on this basis alone, why we have deficit spending? Why we have the deficit and debt we have? Equal? Equitable? Fair? I don't think so. In my humble opinion, I've never understood why states that received so little in return have not revolted in this *spoils system* and advocated to let all states or their respective citizens keep this money and let them decide what to do with it.

The significant observation here to me is if we keep this same type of system, it must be modified to ensure that every state gets a basic return of exchange of one dollar for one dollar. If the system is changed, along with the overall way we tax, let's not collect this money that is given back to the states and let them, the states, keep the taxes in the first place. Let each state determine what amount of tax they want to collect and let each state determine what, where, and how those taxes are allocated or disbursed.

There has been a lot of talk about the federal government going into debt. Most states have a constitutional requirement for a balanced budget. I, for one, believe the federal budget should be balanced and that deficits should be paid off at least the following year they were incurred.

As I've said, the money comes from the people, so why shouldn't it be paid off? We, the people, should pay for policies, products, or services that *we* have incurred. It's not that we don't, as a country, have the money. In my opinion, it's because we've had disingenuous and dishonest cowards as members of Congress.

I wasn't a big fan of President Reagan. He was a fair president, but, especially as his policies pertained to Utah, I wouldn't rank him in the top twenty presidents. I've told friends that I would have ranked him higher if he had decided to raise taxes and/or did away with some of the spending and balanced his budgets under his conservative agenda. I believe that, regardless of the country's economic situation and condition during those years, we could have afforded to pay the bills then, and we should have done so. It's a tragedy now that he, and the Democrats, didn't raise taxes fairly and equitably to reduce the budgets back then. Think what an example—especially for the conservative movement at the time—this would have set for the United States now if Reagan and Congress had then demanded a balanced budget.

Other than during the Depression and World War II, we generally shouldn't have a debt. But from Vietnam onward, I can't see how we couldn't afford to keep and maintain a balanced budget. This includes our three Gulf Wars and the various wars on terrorism.

As I'm trying to get this published, it's now July. I don't know how this latest evolution of the Affordable Care Act and our issue with health care is going to turn out. Let me say however that more than one member of Congress has stated on TV that he's been in contact with his state's governor and other governors.

If we didn't have a Congress, would the states handle this whole process better? You know my answer.

Article VI

HOW IT'S DONE

*The world as we have created it is a process
of our thinking. It cannot be changed
without changing our thinking.*

—*Albert Einstein*

As previously stated, the Founding Fathers had the foresight to include a provision in the Constitution that allowed the document to be amended. They did not write for what reason it should be amended but only that Congress or state legislatures could amend or propose the document should it "deem it necessary" to do so.

I believe that it is now necessary.

What are legislative functions? I'm referring here to what *law making* functions a legislative body has. If at the federal or national level, the law must meet—based on what a reasonable person would concur—one or more of those reasons stated in the preamble:

(1) Forming a more perfect Union
(2) Establishing justice
(3) Ensuring domestic tranquility
(4) Providing for the common defense
(5) Promoting the general welfare
(6) Securing the blessings of liberty

Each bill or proposed law should be required to cite this standard when being proposed, first and upfront, and why this bill or law is therefore needed. If a law can't and doesn't meet any of these criteria, then it shouldn't be passed (or have been passed).

The problem is the difference between a state wanting something versus congressperson X from state Y wanting something.

Related to the above reason for establishing the Constitution, we should consider another part of the story. A very good friend of mine sent me an article that dealt with the old, pre–Civil War idea of state nullification. This is where a state could nullify a federal law if it felt the law was out of line with the state's well-being or if, on its own, the state had determined that the law was unconstitutional. If the state challenged the law on constitutional grounds, then the case was brought before the Supreme Court.

*As Congress takes up the Defense
Department's budget request, lawmakers
scramble to add ships, tanks, and planes
that the military hasn't even asked for.*

—*Bloomberg View, March 3, 2016*

The article my friend sent me is referring to the "supremacy" clause of the Constitution (Article VI), which states, in part, that "This Constitution, and the Laws of the United States which shall be made in Pursuance thereof...shall be the supreme Law of the Land." The article's argument is that many laws were not enacted under the definition of (or in compliance with) the "in Pursuance thereof" criterion.

This is a good area for a spirited discussion. It's clear, at least to me, that the argument about separating from the Union was settled by the Civil War. But as regard to the federal government overreach, however, the tenth article of amendment —as well as federal intrusion into state affairs and the like—brings up very interesting points.

If we do abolish the Congress, then this criterion could be the first thing a state would have to prove before it could offer a new federal bill for consideration and before that bill would become a federal law.

To abolish the Congress—or I should probably state to *replace* the Congress—we only need to reword Article I so that it would be something like, "All federal legislation Powers herein granted shall be vested in the several states' legislatures of the United States."

Utah Senate votes to repeal the 17th Amendment.

—Salt Lake Tribune, February 2016

Now, what of the rest of Article I? Basically, Sections 2 and 3 would no longer be necessary, and Article I would just require some rewording regarding impeachments. The chief justice would still preside for presidential impeachments, but other impeachments would be determined by statute. Appendix A provides a proposal of a reworded and revised Constitution.

Should state legislatures be the federal legislative body, or should that be left to the several states to decide? I could support either way, but for now I'll leave it with the state legislatures. Just to be clear, for example, a state legislature could pass a law that gave that authority and responsibility to its governor. If the state legislature wanted to keep this authority, then this provision could also work. The bottom line is that the state legislature determines how the process works. This method would also keep the tradition of the representative-democracy institution in place.

Appendix C contains data and information on the various states and their legislatures, including each state's size and population. Before you read this, however, please note that I have purposely not included a current version of our Constitution. If you don't already have a copy, you can check one out at the library or look it up online.

What I have attempted to do in appendix B is twofold. First, I tried to combine or insert all the already-passed articles of amendment (A/A) into the basic document, which was a bigger challenge than I anticipated. It may not be constitutionally correct, so please read it with a very critical eye.

I don't know why, after the first ten amendments were passed, the Founders didn't decide to delete or strike through sentences that were amended. To paraphrase Lincoln and his Euclid comment (from the movie), all things that are related should be together on the same article/section of the Constitution.

Second, I tried to remove all the "Congress" parts by either just deleting the phrase or inserting the applicable wording to refer to state legislatures performing this national legislative function. I've used the word "Congregation" in place of "Congress" when referring to the body that meets for the purpose of considering national items of legislative interest. I also envision, when using the word "meeting," that this isn't necessarily a get-together kind of physical meeting but instead should refer to contact, coordination, phone calls, video/Skype, and teleconferencing-type communications 99 percent of the time. I have also used the word "revised" in place of "amended" in order to avoid confusion between what is actually in place now as the law of the land and what I am proposing to replace it with.

Currently, except for Nebraska, all states have a bicameral legislature. The sizes of the legislatures vary along with the sizes of the population they represent. Other than the fact that it (the guarantee that every state shall have a "Republican Form of Government") is contained in the Constitution, both state representatives and senators have to be based on equal representative populations within their respective states. This system was decided by the Supreme Court several decades ago. For what it's worth, I disagree, for a couple of reasons, with that decision.

Basically, if we can have constitutionally unequal representation now in Congress with the states, why shouldn't the states be allowed the same leeway?

People often say that democracy should strive not only to be fair but also to be consistent.

I would disagree with that statement, as I feel it's better and more convenient for citizens to have easily recognizable boundaries to determine political entities. This, to me, is just another inconsistency within our republic. It seems to me that if population for senators isn't based on equal representation throughout the states, then why should representatives also go by population? If Utah is allowed four representatives, then why wouldn't it be just as fair to have all Utahns be allowed to vote for all four? And the logical next step of course would be that all representatives should be representing the same, approximate number of citizens.

Another reason to change the system would be based on the convenience of representation. The gerrymandering of districts is not based on what's good for democracy; it's clearly based on giving the minimum political power to a smaller minority group as a token show of being represented. Gerrymandering has nothing to do with spreading and sharing political ideas, good policy, and diverse voices. It has to do with getting, maintaining, and keeping political power.

Without a Congress, gerrymandering would become moot. Anyway, since we're still a representative democratic republic, I'm staying with using the state legislatures for our federal legislature.

Being a counselor at Boys State—an American Legion program that gives high-school seniors a practical week's application in how our government is supposed to work—I am amazed every year at the number of boys who don't have a clue what "federalism" means or why the word is used when referring to our central, national government. Unfortunately, counselors are not supposed to teach how our federal government works or other aspects of it to include the Constitution. This results in the boys getting three semester hours of political science credit from the university but knowing very little about the Constitution, the federal government, or federalism.

For those who might not want to ask, my short definition of federalism is that it means there is a separation of defined powers—sovereignty—between the states and the federal (central) government. Using a basic, limited reading and understanding of the Constitution, federalism means that the federal government has designated, specific authority; the states have designated, specific authority, as well as any authority and power *not* granted to the federal government; and individual citizens have guaranteed rights (or authority) not otherwise granted to the federal or state governments.

By substituting state legislatures for Congress, these relationships wouldn't change. On the contrary, I would hope those six designated purposes of why we established the Constitution in the first place would be enhanced.

Again, this is not a history lesson, although I remind the readers of George Washington's admonition against political parties. I understand the purpose and reason for lobbyists, PACs, and special interests. I also acknowledge these groups' interests, but I don't think that's what the Founding Fathers were referring to in the phrase "We the People."

With constitutionally granted rights, the individual should be held paramount. I don't believe this is the case with the way the system currently works. The individual, in making up the ever-shrinking middle class, is denied, ignored, and many times discarded by the powerful and moneyed corporations, lobbyists, and special interests. The playing field is not level.

Article VII

HOW WOULD IT WORK?

*Perfection is not attainable, but if we chase
perfection we can catch excellence.*

—*Vince Lombardi*

If we do away with Congress, what mechanism would be used to conduct federal legislative business?

Good question.

There are, to me, many ways this could be accomplished and implemented. I'll offer a few ideas. I admit that these may not be the best, but something this monumental will undoubtedly require some fine-tuning. But please remember that the Founding Fathers didn't get their first approved document right the first time, either. It's still being fine-tuned as we speak.

But I believe it will work better than what's not being done now by our Congress.

> *In the six years of Republican majorities in the House, conservative legislation has gone nowhere because the party can't unify behind anything that might have a chance of passing.*

> —JONATHAN BERNSTEIN, WASHINGTON POST, SEPTEMBER 15, 2016

The first way—easy, simple, direct, and fast—is to turn federal legislative business over to the state legislatures or to governors. Governors are elected by the state (whatever part of the electorate that decides to vote). When governors, by themselves or from other sources, determine that some federal statute needs to be changed, updated, revised, or whatever, then they propose the change to the other states. Governors may or may not consult with their own legislatures.

> *Debt problem, the budget, a defense bill, and a Supreme Court nominee.*

> —SALT LAKE TRIBUNE, MAY 29, 2016

Depending on what majority vote is required (simple majority, two-thirds, or three-quarters), if the governor obtains that requirement from the other states, then the law is passed and forwarded to the president for signature. The current processing rules are still pertinent.

Who writes the law? If governors do this, then they determine how large a staff they need to write the law. I mention this because I believe that many, if not most, of the laws that are currently written are not done by actual legislators but by their staff, lobbyists, PACs, businesses, corporations, and other special-interest groups.

A second possible way is to turn federal legislative business over to the state legislatures. The same processes of how state laws are proposed will pertain in this case, where the governor's signature will still be required (unless a veto is overridden). Per appendix C, there are over 7,000 state legislators, so isn't this better than just some 535 members now in Congress as a representative democracy?

A third way could be that states would be permitted to design their own "federal legislative office" for this function or purpose. Such an office could be under the supervision of either the governor or the legislature or a combination of both.

A fourth way could follow that old Marine saying for new second lieutenants: "Lieutenant, lead, follow, or get the hell out of the way." That is, designate whichever states the president and the vice president are from as the "lead" states for national legislation. Here's a thought: give the VP a real job since he's already, constitutionally, the only member of two branches of government. That way, the VP would be the person in charge of overseeing the processing of federal bills and laws between the states. For those who don't remember, the VP already oversees the Senate (although the VP doesn't have a vote, unless there's a tie), since the Constitution also designates the vice president of the United States as the president of the Senate.

For those who don't like Washington, DC, and think the federal government is always getting into local affairs where it doesn't belong or that government is too big and should be curtailed and starved, then this process should make them ecstatic. This method should also be supported by die-hard states' rights advocates (Utah has many) and strong supporters of the Tenth Amendment. This would also negate the feeling that once people get to Congress, they get that lobotomy that changes them from a "state" person to an alien "federal" person. If states could now make federal laws, then those laws would clearly be for the benefit of all, if not most, of the states and the Union as a whole.

*IRS chief wants his rights protected
in House impeachment inquiry.*

—Salt Lake Tribune, September 20, 2016

Another reason for this change is that none of those Washington bureaucrats would be back there thinking up ways of taking away more of the states' rights.

It has always surprised me when I hear people say that once people get into Congress, their DNA immediately goes from state to federal. It matters not when I ask them who has reelected this person or where does this person come from. It's as if all the federal statutes that we have ever passed were done by people who'd never lived in any of these states.

It's always Washington's fault or some alien 'federal' person, regardless of who proposed the law or who voted in the majority for it or that the president wasn't from a state.

Why is it that we can solve many of the mysteries God gives us—chemistry, flight, physics, the cosmos, the moon, Mars—but we can't solve mysteries and problems we create ourselves?

As I tried to finally finish up the ending to this manuscript in September 2016, I had some hope that Congress would do credit to itself by doing what's right. I would have bet against Congress, but I was partially right that Congress did, as of September 28, pass a bill to avoid a government shutdown. Technically it was a "temporary spending bill" that was only good through December 9.

Of course, it was an election year, and neither side wanted to chance taking the blame or (more importantly) the losses during the election. So my argument still stands that Congress undertook these negotiations and compromises only because of political considerations and not because of any obligations of duty, the oaths they took, or the theory that they should put the national interest first.

On September 6, Norman Ornstein wrote a piece in the *Washington Post* headlined "Republicans' Devotion to Obstructionism Backfired." In it, he wrote about how the Republicans wanted to obstruct President Obama at every turn because that approach worked in off-election years, but it backfired in 2012. He took Tom Korologus and Richard Allen to task for their recent (at the time) op-ed in which their advice to the GOP was to concede the elections and start to work toward 2018 and 2020. But their advice wasn't to start taking back the party to solve the broad and real challenges and problems facing the country—no. Their advice was to double down on obstructionist approaches, "gotcha" investigations, and the blocking of Supreme Court nominees.

Is this what I have to look forward to? The next president's ending to the State of the Union should not be "God bless America" but "God help America." It's hard to think or say how someone might have thought some two hundred years ago. At least George Will tried in his *Washington Post* piece on September 26, titled "Donald Trump's Rise Reflects America's Decay."

I loved his comparison of Trump to Spain's Ferdinand III, when the king vowed to end "the disastrous mania of thinking." Will believes that the constitutional Founders wanted more than anything limited government under the philosophy that government was instituted to secure preexisting natural rights.

I believe that the Founders would today support doing away with Congress. We no longer need these middlemen, and they serve no useful purpose. I don't want another thirty years of this; I've had enough. The Founders gave the president the right to ask Congress for legislation (Article II, Section 3), and it seems we don't ask Congress to do this because we wait to see what the presidential candidate wants to do. It seems logical to me to now just let the president and vice president directly ask the states for legislation.

It's time "We the People" took back the high ideals, principles, and goals of what these United States have always stood for.

The August 4, 2017 issue of The Week reprinted an excerpt from a book called Raven Rock: The Story of the U.S. Government's Secret Plan to Save Itself-While the Rest of Us Die. It deals with plans to keep the government functioning after catastrophic nuclear attack during the Reagan era. One of the questions that came up was whether to reconstitute Congress. Years later, a participant recalled "It was decided that no, it would be easier to operate without them."

It's time to get it right.

This is my proposal. If you don't like it or have something better to offer, please throw your idea on the table.

APPENDIX A: POSSIBLE REVISED CONSTITUTION OF THE UNITED STATES

(Note: Some modern updating has been done in regard to grammar, punctuation, and spelling.)

We the People of the United States, in Order to form a more perfect Union, establish Justice, ensure domestic Tranquility, provide for the common Defense, promote the general Welfare, and secure the Blessings of Liberty to ourselves and our Posterity, do ordain and establish this Constitution of the United States of America.

ARTICLE I

SECTION 1

All legislative Powers herein granted shall be vested in a Congregation of the Legislatures of the several states, which shall consist of a State Senate and a State House of Representatives.

SECTION 2

The actual Enumeration (National census) shall be made in the first year at the start of every decade while Electors still choose the President.

14TH A/A, SECTION 2

Electors shall be apportioned among the several states according to their respective numbers, counting the whole number of persons in each state, excluding Indians not taxed. But when the right to vote at any election for the choice of electors for President and Vice President of the United States, the Executive and Judicial officers of a State, or the members of the Legislature thereof, is denied to any of the male inhabitants of such State, being twenty-one years of age, and citizens of the United States, or in any way abridged, except for participation in rebellion, or other crime, the basis of representation therein shall be reduced in the proportion which the number of such male citizens shall bear to the whole number of male citizens twenty-one years of age in such State.

SECTION 3

The several States' Senates of the United States shall act as the Senate of the United States.

The States' Senates shall choose their own officers. The States' Senates shall have the sole Power to try all Impeachments. When sitting for the Purpose, they shall be on Oath or Affirmation. When the President of the United States is tried, the Chief Justice shall preside, and no Person shall be convicted without the Concurrence of two-thirds of the Members.

Judgment in Cases of Impeachment shall not extend further than to removal from Office, and disqualification to hold and enjoy any Office of honor, Trust, or Profit under the United States, but the Party convicted shall nevertheless be liable and subject to Indictment, Trial, Judgment, and Punishment, according to Law.

SECTION 4

The Times, Places, and Manner of holding Elections for State Senators and State Representatives shall be prescribed in each State by the Legislature thereof, but the Congregation legislature of the United States may at any time by Law make or alter such Regulations.

20TH A/A, SECTION 2

The Congregation shall assemble at least once in every year, and such Meeting shall begin at noon on the third day of January, unless the Congregation shall by law appoint a different day.

SECTION 5

Each House in the several States shall be the Judge of the Elections, Returns, and Qualifications of its own Members, and a Majority of each shall constitute a Quorum to do Business; but a smaller Number may adjourn from day to day and may be authorized to compel the Attendance of absent Members in such Manner, and under such Penalties, as each House may provide.

Each House in the several States may determine the Rules of its Proceedings, punish its Members for disorderly Behavior, and, with the Concurrence of two-thirds, expel a Member.

Each House shall keep a journal of its Proceedings and from time to time publish the same, excepting such Parts as may in their Judgment require Secrecy, and the Yeas and Nays of the Members of either House on any question shall, at the Desire of one-fifth of those Present, be entered on the Journal.

Neither House in the several States, during the Session of Congregation, shall, without the Consent of the other, adjourn for more than three days, nor to any other Place than that in which the two Houses shall be sitting.

SECTION 6

The Senators and Representatives shall receive a Compensation for their Services, to be ascertained by State Law, by their respective State Legislatures. They shall in all Cases, except Treason, Felony, and Breach of the Peace, be privileged from Arrest during their Attendance at the Session of their respective Houses and in going to and returning from the same; and, for any Speech or Debate in either House, they shall not be questioned in any other Place.

No Senator or Representative shall, during the Time for which he or she was elected, be appointed to any civil Office under the Authority of the United States that shall have been created, or the Emoluments whereof shall have been increased, during such time; and no Person holding any Office under the United States shall be a Member of either House during his or her Continuance in Office.

SECTION 7

All Bills for raising Revenue shall originate in a State House of the several States, but the State Senates may propose or concur with Amendments as on other Bills.

Every Bill that shall have passed a House of the several States and the State Senates shall, before it becomes a Law, be presented to the President of the United States; the President, if approving, shall sign it, but if not, the President shall return it along with the Objections to that House in which it has originated, which shall then enter the Objections at large on their Journal and proceed to reconsider it. If after such Reconsideration two-thirds of that House shall agree to pass the Bill, it shall be sent, together with the Objections, to the Senates of the several States, by which it shall likewise be reconsidered, and if approved by two-thirds of that House, it shall become a Law. But in all such Cases, the Votes of both Houses of the several States shall be determined by Yeas and Nays, and the Names of the Persons voting for and against the Bill shall be entered on the Journal of each House respectively. If any Bill shall not be returned by the President within ten Days (Sundays excepted) after it shall have been presented to the President, the Same shall be a Law, in like Manner as if the President had signed it, unless the Congregation by its Adjournment prevents its Return, in which Case it shall not be a Law.

Every Order, Resolution, or Vote to which the Concurrence of the Senates and Houses of Representatives may be necessary (except on a question of Adjournment) shall be presented to the President of the United States, and before the Same shall take Effect, shall be approved by the President; or, if disapproved, it shall be repassed by two-thirds of the Senates and the Houses of Representatives of the several States, according to the Rules and Limitations prescribed in the Case of a Bill.

SECTION 8

The Congregation shall have Power to lay and collect Taxes, Duties, Imposts, and Excises to pay the Debts and provide for the common Defense and general Welfare of the United States, but all Duties, Imposts, and Excises shall be uniform throughout the United States:

* to borrow Money on the credit of the United States;
* to regulate Commerce with foreign Nations, and among the several States, and with the Indian Tribes;
* to establish a uniform Rule of Naturalization and uniform Laws on the subject of Bankruptcies throughout the United States;
* to coin Money, regulate the Value thereof (and of foreign Coin), and fix the Standard of Weights and Measures;
* to provide for the Punishment of counterfeiting the Securities and current Coin of the United States;
* to establish Post Offices and post Roads;
* to promote the Progress of Science and useful Arts by securing for limited Times to Authors and Inventors the exclusive Right to their respective Writings and Discoveries;
* to constitute Tribunals inferior to the Supreme Court;
* to define and punish Piracies and Felonies committed on the high Seas, and Offenses against the Law of Nations;
* to declare War, grant Letters of Reprisal, and make Rules concerning Captures on Land and Water;
* to raise and support Armies (but no Appropriation of Money to that Use shall be for a longer Term than two Years);
* to provide and maintain a Navy;

* to make Rules for the Government and Regulation of the land and naval Forces;

* to provide for calling forth the Militia to execute the Laws of the Union, suppress Insurrections, and repel Invasions;

* to provide for organizing, arming, and disciplining the Militia and for governing such Part of them as may be employed in the Service of the United States, reserving to the States respectively the Appointment of the Officers and the Authority of training the Militia according to the discipline prescribed by the Congregation;

* to exercise exclusive Legislation in all Cases whatsoever, over such District (not exceeding ten Miles square) as may, by Cession of particular States and the Acceptance of Congregation, become the Seat of the Government of the United States, and to exercise like Authority over all Places purchased by the Consent of the Legislature of the State in which the Same shall be, for the Erection of Forts, Magazines, Arsenals, Dock yards, and other needful Buildings; and to make all Laws necessary and proper for carrying into Execution the foregoing Powers and all other Powers vested by this Constitution in the Government of the United States or in any Department or Officer thereof.

SECTION 9

The Migration or Importation of such Persons as any of the States now existing shall think proper to admit shall not be prohibited by the Congregation prior to the Year 1808, but a Tax or duty may be imposed on such Importation, not exceeding ten dollars for each Person.

The Privilege of the Writ of Habeas Corpus shall not be suspended, unless when in Cases of Rebellion or Invasion the public Safety may require.

No Bill of Attainder or ex post facto Law shall be passed.

No Capitation or other direct Tax shall be laid, unless in Proportion to the Census or Enumeration herein before directed to be taken.

16TH A/A

The Congregation has the power to lay and collect taxes on incomes, from whatever source derived, without apportionment among the several States, and without regard to any census or enumeration.

No Tax or Duty shall be laid on articles exported from any State.

No Preference shall be given by any Regulation of Commerce or Revenue to the Ports of one State over those of another, nor shall Vessels bound to, or from, one State be obliged to enter, clear, or pay Duties in another.

No Money shall be drawn from the Treasury but in Consequence of Appropriations made by Law, and a regular Statement and Account of the Receipts and Expenditures of all public Money shall be published from time to time.

No Title of Nobility shall be granted by the United States, and no Person holding any Office of Profit or Trust under them shall, without the Consent of the Congregation, accept any present, Emolument, Office, or Title of any kind whatever, from any Sovereign or foreign State.

SECTION 10

No State shall enter into any Treaty, Alliance, or Confederation; grant Letters of Reprisal; coin Money; emit Bills of Credit; make anything but gold and silver Coin a Tender in Payment of Debts; pass any Bill of Attainder, ex post facto Law, or Law impairing the Obligation of Contracts; or grant any Title of Nobility.

No State shall, without the Consent of the Congregation, lay any Imposts or Duties on Imports or Exports, except what may be absolutely necessary for executing its inspection Laws; the net Produce of all Duties and Imposts laid by any State on Imports or Exports shall be for the Use of the Treasury of the United States, and all such Laws shall be subject to the Revision and Control of the Congregation.

No State shall, without the Consent of the Congregation, lay any Duty of Tonnage, keep Troops or Ships of War in time of Peace, enter into any Agreement or Compact with another State or with a foreign Power, or engage in War unless actually invaded or in such imminent Danger as will not admit of delay.

ARTICLE II

SECTION 1

The executive Power shall be vested in a President of the United States of America, who shall hold Office during the Term of four Years, and, together with the Vice President, chosen for the same Term, be elected as follows.

Each State shall appoint, in such Manner as the Legislature thereof may direct, a Number of Electors equal to the whole Number to which the State may be entitled in the old way as a National Congress was still in effect based on the Census every ten years, but no State Senator or Representative, or Person holding an Office of Trust or Profit under the United States, shall be appointed an Elector.

23RD A/A

Section 1. The District constituting the seat of government of the United States shall appoint in such manner as the Congregation may direct:

A number of electors of President and Vice President equal to the whole number of Senators and Representatives in Congregation to which the District would be entitled if it were a state, but in no event more than the least populous state; they shall be in addition to those appointed by the states, but they shall be considered, for the purposes of the election of President and Vice President, to be electors appointed by a state; and they shall meet in the District and perform such duties as provided by the twelfth article of amendment.

Section 2. The Congregation shall have power to enforce this article by appropriate legislation.

12TH A/A

The Electors shall meet in their respective states and vote by ballot for President and Vice President, one of whom, at least, shall not be an inhabitant of the same state with themselves; they shall name in their ballots the person voted for as President, and in distinct ballots the person voted for as Vice President, and they shall make distinct lists of all persons voted for as President, and of all persons voted for as Vice President, and of the number of votes for each, which lists they shall sign and certify and transmit sealed to the seat of the government of the United States, directed to the President of the Congregation Senate.

The President of the Congregation shall, in the presence of the whole Congregation, open all the certificates, and the votes shall then be counted. The person having the greatest Number of votes for President shall be the President, if such number be a majority of the whole number of Electors appointed, and if no person has such majority, then, from the persons having the highest numbers not exceeding three on the list of those voted for as President, the Congregation House of Representatives shall choose immediately, by ballot, the President. But in choosing the President, the votes shall be taken by states, the representation from each state having one vote; a quorum for this purpose shall consist of a member or members from two-thirds of the states, and a majority of all the states shall be necessary for a choice.

And if the Congregation House of Representatives shall not choose a President whenever the right of choice shall devolve upon them, before the fourth day of March next following, then the Vice President shall act as President, as in the case of the death or other constitutional disability of the President. The person having the greatest number of votes as Vice President shall be the Vice President, if such number be a majority of the whole number of Electors appointed, and if no person has a majority, then, from the two highest numbers on the list, the Congregation Senate shall choose the Vice President. A quorum for the purpose shall consist of two-thirds of the whole number of Congregation Senators, and a majority of the whole number shall be necessary for a choice. But no person constitutionally ineligible to the office of Present shall be eligible to that of Vice President of the United States.

The Congregation may determine the Time of choosing the Electors and the Day on which they shall give their Votes; this Day shall be the same throughout the United States.

No Person except a natural-born Citizen or a Citizen of the United States at the time of the Adoption of this Constitution shall be eligible to the Office of President, neither shall any person be eligible to that Office who shall not have attained the Age of thirty-five Years and been fourteen Years a Resident within the United States.

20TH A/A
Section 1
The terms of the President and Vice President shall end at noon on the twentieth day of January, and the terms of their successors shall then begin.

[Section 2 incorporated into Article I, Section 4]
Section 3
If, at the time fixed for the beginning of the term of the President, the President elect shall have died, the Vice President elect shall

become President. If a President shall not have been chosen before the time fixed for the beginning of the President's term, or if the President elect shall have failed to qualify, then the Vice President elect shall act as President until a President shall have qualified. The Congregation may by law provide for the case wherein neither a President elect nor a Vice President elect shall have qualified, declaring who shall then act as President, or the manner in which one who is to act shall be selected, and such person shall act accordingly until a President or Vice President shall have qualified.

Section 4

The States may by law provide for the case of the death of any of the persons from whom their House of Representatives may choose a President whenever the right of choice shall have devolved upon them, and for the case of the death of any of the persons from whom the Congregation Senate may choose a Vice President whenever the right of choice shall have devolved upon them.

Section 5

Sections 1 and 2 shall take effect on the fifteenth day of October following the ratification of this article.

Section 6

This article shall be inoperative unless it shall have been ratified as an amendment to the Constitution by the legislatures of three-fourths of the several States within seven years from the date of its submission.

25TH A/A

Section 1

In case of the removal of the President from office or of the President's death or resignation, the Vice President shall become President.

Section 2

Whenever there is a vacancy in the office of the Vice President, the President shall nominate a Vice President, who shall take office upon confirmation by a majority vote of both Houses of the Congregation.

Section 3

Whenever the President transmits to the President pro tempore of the Congregation Senate and the Speaker of the Congregation House of Representatives the President's written declaration of inability to discharge the powers and duties of office, and until the President transmits to the President pro tempore of the Congregation Senate and the Speaker of the Congregation House of Representatives a written declaration to the contrary, such powers and duties shall be discharged by the Vice President as Acting President.

Section 4

Whenever the Vice President and a majority of either the principal officers of the executive departments or of such other body as the Congregation may by law provide transmit to the President pro tempore of the Congregation Senate and the Speaker of the House of Representatives their written declaration that the

President is unable to discharge the powers and duties of office, the Vice President shall immediately assume the powers and duties of the office as Acting President. Thereafter, when the President transmits to the President pro tempore and Speaker written declaration that no inability exists, the President shall resume the powers and duties of office unless the Vice President and a majority of either the principal officers of the executive department or of such other body as the Congregation may by law provide transmit within four days to the President Pro Tempore and Speaker their written declaration that the President is unable to discharge the powers and duties of office.

Thereupon the Congregation shall decide the issue, assembling within forty-eight hours for that purpose (if not in session). If the Congregation, within twenty-one days after receipt of the latter written declaration (or, if Congregation is not in session within twenty-one days after the Congregation is required to assemble), determines by two-thirds vote of both Houses that the President is unable to discharge the powers and duties of office, the Vice President shall continue to discharge the same as Acting President; otherwise, the President shall resume the powers and duties of office.

The President shall, at stated Times, receive a Compensation that shall neither be increased nor diminished during the Period for which the President shall have been elected, and the President shall not receive within that Period any other Emolument from the United States or any of the individual States.

Before the President enters on the Execution of Office, the following Oath or Affirmation must be taken: "I do solemnly swear that I will faithfully execute the Office of President of the

United States and will, to the best of my Ability, preserve, protect, and defend the Constitution of the United States."

SECTION 2

The President shall be Commander in Chief of the Army and Navy of the United States and of the Militia of the several States, when called into the actual Service of the United States; the President may require the Opinion, in writing, of the principal Officer in each of the executive Departments upon any Subject relating to the Duties of their respective Offices, and the President shall have Power to grant Reprieves and Pardons for Offenses against the United States, except in Cases of Impeachment.

The President shall have Power, by and with the Advice and Consent of the State Senates, to make Treaties, provided two-thirds of the Senators present concur; and the President shall nominate and, by and with the Advice and Consent of the State Senates, shall appoint Ambassadors, other public Ministers and Consuls, Judges of the Supreme Court, and all other Officers of the United States whose Appointments are not herein otherwise provided for and that shall be established by Law: but the Congregation may by Law vest the Appointment of such inferior Officers, as they think proper, in the President alone, in the Courts of Law, or in the Heads of Departments.

The President shall have Power to fill all Vacancies that may happen during the Recesses of the State Senates by granting Commissions, which shall expire at the End of their next Session.

SECTION 3

The President shall from time to time give to the Congregation Information of the State of the Union and recommend to the Congregation's Consideration such Measures as shall be judged necessary and expedient; the President may, on extraordinary Occasions, convene the Congregation as a whole (or either of the States' separate Houses) and, in Case of Disagreement between them with Respect to the Time of Adjournment, the President may adjourn these bodies to such Time as shall be proper; the President shall receive Ambassadors and other public Ministers, shall take Care that the Laws be faithfully executed, and shall Commission all the Officers of the United States.

SECTION 4

The President, Vice President, and all civil Officers of the United States shall be removed from Office on Impeachment for, and Conviction of, Treason, Bribery, or other high Crimes and Misdemeanors.

22ND A/A

Section 1. No person shall be elected to the office of the President more than twice, and no person who has held the office of President, or acted as President, for more than two years of a term to which some other person was elected more than once shall be elected to the office of the President more than once. But this article shall not apply to any person holding the office of President when this article was proposed by the Congress, and shall not prevent any person who may be holding the office of President, or acting as President, during the term within which this article becomes operative from holding the office of President or acting as President during the remainder of such term.

Section 2. This article shall be inoperative unless it shall have been ratified as an amendment to the Constitution by the legislatures of three-fourths of the several states within seven years from the date of its submission to the states by the Congress.

ARTICLE III

SECTION 1

The judicial Power of the United States shall be vested in one Supreme Court and in such inferior Courts as the Congregation may from time to time ordain and establish. The Judges, both of the Supreme and Inferior Courts, shall hold their Officers during good Behavior and shall, at stated Times, receive for their Services a Compensation that shall not be diminished during their Continuance in Office.

SECTION 2

The judicial Power shall extend, to all Cases in Law and Equity arising under this Constitution, the Laws of the United States and Treaties made (or that shall be made) under their Authority; to all Cases affecting Ambassadors, other public Ministers, and Consuls; to all Cases of admiralty and maritime Jurisdiction; to Controversies to which the United States shall be a Party; and to Controversies between two or more States, between Citizens of different States, and between Citizens of the same State claiming Lands under Grants of different States.

11TH A/A

The Judicial power of the United States shall not be construed to extend to any suit in law or equity, commenced or prosecuted against one of the United States by Citizens of another State, or by Citizens or Subjects of any Foreign State.

In all Cases affecting Ambassadors, other public Ministers, and Consuls, and those in which a State shall be Party, the

Supreme Court shall have original Jurisdiction. In all the other Cases before mentioned, the Supreme Court shall have appellate Jurisdiction, both as to Law and Fact, with such Exceptions, and under such Regulations, as the Congregation shall make.

The Trial of all Crimes, except in Cases of Impeachment, shall be by Jury, and such Trials shall be held in the State where the said Crimes shall have been committed; when not committed within any State, the Trial shall be at such Place or Places as the Congregation may by Law have directed.

SECTION 3

Treason against the United States shall consist only in levying War against the States and in adhering to the United States' Enemies by giving them Aid and Comfort. No Person shall be convicted of Treason unless on the Testimony of two Witnesses to the same overt Act, or on Confession in open Court. The Congregation shall have Power to declare the Punishment of Treason, but no Attainder of Treason shall work Corruption of Blood or Forfeiture, except during the Life of the Person attainted.

ARTICLE IV

SECTION 1

Full Faith and Credit shall be given in each State to the public Acts, Records, and judicial Proceedings of every other State, and the Congregation may by general Laws prescribe the Manner in which such Acts, Records, and Proceedings shall be proved, as well as the Effect thereof.

SECTION 2

The Citizens of each State shall be entitled to all Privileges and Immunities of Citizens in the several States. A Person charged in any State with Treason, Felony, or other Crime who shall flee from Justice and be found in another State shall, on Demand of the executive Authority of the State from which the person fled, be delivered up, to be removed to the State having Jurisdiction of the Crime.

13TH A/A

Neither slavery nor involuntary servitude, except as a punishment for crime whereof the party shall have been duly convicted, shall exist within the United States, or any place subject to the United States' jurisdiction.

14TH A/A

Section 1

All persons born or naturalized in the United States, and subject to the jurisdiction thereof, are citizens of the United States and of the State wherein they reside. No State shall make or enforce any law that shall abridge the privileges or immunities of citizens of the United States, nor shall any State deprive any person of life, liberty, or property without due process of law, nor deny to any person within its jurisdiction the equal protection of the law.

[Section 2 incorporated into Article I, Section 2]
Section 3
No person shall be an elector of President and Vice President (or hold any office—civil or military—under the United States or under any State) who, having previously taken an oath as a member of Congress or as an officer of the United States (or as a member of any State legislature or as an executive or judicial officer of any State) to support the Constitution of the United States, shall have engaged in insurrection or rebellion against the same, or given aid or comfort to the enemies thereof. But the Congregation may by a vote of two-thirds of each House remove such disability.

Section 4
The validity of the public debt of the United States authorized by law—including debts incurred for payment of pensions and bounties for services in suppressing insurrection or rebellion—shall not be questioned. But neither the United States nor any State shall assume or pay any debt or obligation incurred in and of insurrection or rebellion against the United States or any claim for the loss or emancipation of any slave, but all such debts, obligations, and claims shall be held illegal and void.

Section 5
The Congregation shall have power to enforce, by appropriate legislation, the provisions of this article.

15TH A/A

The right of citizens of the United States to vote shall not be denied or abridged by the United States or by any State on account of race, color, or previous condition of servitude.

19TH A/A

The right of citizens of the United States to vote shall not be denied or abridged by the United States or by any State on account of sex.

24TH A/A

The right of citizens of the United States to vote in any primary or other election for President or Vice President, for electors for President or Vice President, shall not be denied or abridged by the United States or any State by reason of failure to pay any poll tax or other tax.

26TH A/A

The right of citizens of the United States who are eighteen years of age or older to vote shall not be denied or abridged by the United States or by any State on account of age.

SECTION 3

New States may be admitted by the Congregation into this Union, but no new State shall be formed or erected within the Jurisdiction of any other State, nor any State be formed by the Junction of Two or more States, or Parts of States, without the Consent of the Legislatures of the States concerned as well as of the Congregation.

The Congregation shall have Power to dispose of and make all needful Rules and Regulations respecting the Territory or other Property belonging to the United States, and nothing in this Constitution shall be so construed as to Prejudice any Claims of the United States or of any particular State.

SECTION 4

The United States shall guarantee to every State in this Union a Republican Form of Government and shall protect each of the States against Invasion; and, on Application of the Legislature, or of the Executive (when the Legislature cannot be convened), against domestic Violence.

ARTICLE V

The Congregation, whenever two-thirds of both Houses in each State shall deem it necessary, shall propose Amendments to this Constitution—or, on the Application of the Legislatures of two-thirds of the several States, shall call a Convention for proposing Amendments—that, in either Case, shall be valid to all Intents and Purposes as Part of this Constitution, when ratified by the Legislatures of three-fourths of the several States, or by Conventions in three-fourths thereof, as the one or the other Mode of Ratification may be proposed by the Congregation, provided that no Amendment that may be made prior to the Year 1808 shall in any Manner affect the first and fourth Clauses in the Ninth Section of the first Article.

ARTICLE VI

All Debts contracted and Engagements entered into before the Adoption of this Constitution shall be as valid against the United States under this Constitution as under the Confederation.

This Constitution, and the Laws of the United States that shall be made in Pursuance thereof, and all Treaties made, or that shall be made, under the Authority of the United States, shall be the supreme Law of the Land; the Judges in every State shall be bound thereby, anything in the Constitution or Laws of any State to the Contrary notwithstanding.

The Members of the several State Legislatures, and all executive and judicial Officers, both of the United States and of the several States, shall be bound by Oath or Affirmation to support this Constitution, but no religious Test shall ever be required as a Qualification to any Office or public Trust under the United States.

ARTICLE VII

The Ratification of the Conventions of nine States shall be sufficient for the Establishment of this Constitution between the States so ratifying the Same.

Done in Convention by the Unanimous Consent of the States present the seventeenth Day of September in the Year of our Lord 1787 and of the Independence of the United States of America the Twelfth in Witness whereof We have hereunto subscribed our Names,

Geo. Washington—President
and deputy from Virginia
And signed by members of the other States,
Attest William Jackson Secretary

APPENDIX B: ARTICLES IN ADDITION TO, AND AMENDMENT OF, THE CONSTITUTION OF THE UNITED STATES

The first ten Amendments, known as the Bill of Rights, were proposed by the Congress on September 25, 1789; ratification by the states was completed on December 15, 1791.

1ST A/A

Congress shall make no law respecting an establishment of religion, or prohibiting the free exercise thereof, or abridging the freedom of speech, or of the press, or the right of the people peaceably to assemble, and to petition the Government for a redress of grievances.

2ND A/A

A well-regulated Militia, being necessary to the security of a free State, and the right of the people to keep and bear Arms, shall not be infringed.

3RD A/A

No Soldier shall, in time of peace, be quartered in any house without the consent of the Owner, nor in time of war but in a manner to be prescribed by law.

4TH A/A

The right of the people to be secure in their persons, houses, papers, and effects against unreasonable searches and seizures shall not be violated, and no Warrants shall issue but upon probable cause, supported by Oath or affirmation, and particularly describing the place to be searched and the persons or things to be seized.

5TH A/A

No person shall be held to answer for a capital, or otherwise infamous, crime, unless on a presentment or indictment of a Grand Jury, except in cases arising in the land or naval forces, or in the Militia, when in actual service in time of War or public danger; nor shall any person be subject for the same offence to be twice put in jeopardy of life or limb; nor shall people be compelled in any criminal case to be witness against themselves, nor be deprived of life, liberty, or property, without due process of law; nor shall private property be taken for public use without just compensation.

6TH A/A

In all criminal prosecutions, the accused shall enjoy the right to a speedy and public trial by an impartial jury of the State and district wherein the crime shall have been committed, which district shall have been previously ascertained by law, and to be informed of the nature and cause of the accusation, to be confronted with the witnesses against the accused, to have compulsory process for obtaining Witnesses in the accused's favor, and to have the assistance of counsel for the accused's defense.

7TH A/A

In Suits at common law where the value in controversy shall exceed twenty dollars, the right of trial by jury shall be preserved, and no fact tried by a jury shall be otherwise reexamined in any Court of the United States than according to the rules of common law.

8TH A/A
Excessive bail shall not be required, nor excessive fines imposed, nor cruel and unusual punishments inflicted.

9TH A/A
The enumeration in the Constitution of certain rights shall not be construed to deny or disparage others retained by the people.

10TH A/A
The powers not delegated to the United States by the Constitution, nor prohibited by it to the States, are reserved to the States respectively, or to the people.

11TH A/A - Proposed by Congress on March 4, 1794;
    declared ratified by the states on January 8, 1798;
    incorporated into Article III, Section 2.

12TH A/A - Proposed by Congress on December 9, 1803;
    declared ratified by the states on September 25, 1804;
    incorporated into Article II, Section 1.

13TH A/A - Proposed by Congress January 31, 1865;
    declared ratified by the states on December 18, 1865;
    incorporated into Article IV, Section 2.

14TH A/A (SECTIONS 1-5)
> Proposed by Congress on June 13, 1866;
> declared ratified by the states on July 28, 1868;
> Sections 1, 3, 4, & 5 incorporated into Article IV, Section 2;
> Section 2 incorporated into Article I, Section 2.]

15TH A/A - Proposed by Congress on February 26, 1869;
> declared ratified by the states on March 30, 1870;
> incorporated into Article IV, Section 2.

16TH A/A - Proposed by Congress on July 12, 1909;
> declared ratified by the states on February 25, 1913;
> incorporated into Article I, Section 9.

17TH A/A (POPULAR ELECTION OF SENATORS)
> Proposed by Congress on May 13, 1912;
> declared ratified by the states on May 31, 1913;
> article repealed, because revisions to the Constitution would abolish representatives and senators.

18TH A/A (INTOXICATING LIQUORS)
> Proposed by Congress on December 18, 1918;
> declared ratified by the states on January 29, 1919;
> article repealed by the Twenty-First Amendment, which prohibited intoxicating liquors.

19TH A/A - Proposed by Congress on June 4, 1919;
             declared ratified by the states on August 26, 1920;
             incorporated into Article IV, Section 2.

20TH A/A (SECTIONS 1-6)
             Proposed by Congress on March 2, 1932;
             declared ratified by the states on February 6, 1933;
             Sections 1 & 3-6 incorporated into Article II, Section 1;
             Section 2 incorporated into Article I, Section 4.

21ST A/A - Proposed by Congress February 20, 1933;
             declared ratified by the states on December 5, 1933.
             This article repealed the Eighteenth Amendment,
             which dealt with the prohibition of liquors.]

22ND A/A - Proposed by Congress March 21, 1947;
             declared ratified by the states on March 1, 1951;
             incorporated into Article II, Section 4.

23RD A/A - Proposed by Congress June 17, 1960;
             declared ratified by the states on March 29, 1961;
             incorporated into Article II, Section 1.

24TH A/A - Proposed by Congress on August 27, 1962;
             declared ratified by the states February 4, 1964;
             incorporated into Article IV, Section 2.

25TH A/A - Proposed by Congress on July 6, 1956;
    declared ratified by the states February 23, 1967;
    incorporated into Article II, Section 1.

26TH A/A - Proposed by Congress on March 23, 1971;
    declared ratified by the states July 5, 1971;
    incorporated into Article IV, Section 2.

27TH A/A (COMPENSATION FOR SENATORS AND REPRESENTATIVES)
    Proposed by James Madison in 1789;
    certified as valid by the archivist of the United States
    May 18, 1992;
    better late than never: this article would be repealed,
    because representatives and senators would be abol-
    ished by the revised Constitution.

APPENDIX C: THE FIFTY STATES AND WASHINGTON, DC, BY GROUPINGS

EAST, MIDDLE, AND WEST GROUPINGS

Arranged by: (1) state; (2) electoral votes; (3) population (millions [2011]); (4) land (thousand square miles); (5) members in the state legislature.

East					Middle					West				
1	2	3	4	5	1	2	3	4	5	1	2	3	4	5
DE	3	0.898	1.9	62	LA	8	4.5	43.5	144	CA	55	37.3	155.9	100
PA	20	12.7	44.8	253	IN	11	6.5	35.8	150	NV	6	2.7	109.8	63
NJ	14	8.8	7.4	120	MS	6	3	46.9	174	NE	5	1.8	76.8	63
GA	16	9.7	57.9	236	IL	20	12.8	55.5	177	CO	9	5	103.7	100
CT	7	3.6	4.8	187	AL	9	4.8	50.7	135	KS	6	2.9	81.8	165
MA	11	6.5	7.8	200	KY	8	4.3	39.7	138	ND	3	0.673	68.9	141
MD	10	5.8	9.7	188	MO	10	6	68.8	197	SD	3	0.814	75.8	105
SC	9	4.6	30.1	170	AR	6	2.9	52	135	MT	3	0.989	145.5	150
NH	4	1.3	8.9	424	MI	16	9.9	56.8	138	WA	12	6.7	16.5	147
VA	13	8	39.5	140	TN	11	6.3	41.2	132	ID	4	1.6	82.7	105
NY	29	19.4	47.2	213	TX	38	25.1	261.7	181	WY	3	0.564	97.1	90
NC	15	9.5	48.7	170	IA	6	3	55.8	150	UT	6	2.8	82.1	104
RI	4	1	1.04	113	WI	10	5.7	54.3	132	OR	7	3.8	68.6	149
VT	3	0.626	9.2	180	OK	7	3.8	68.6	149	NM	5	2	121.3	112
ME	4	1.3	30.8	186	MN	10	5.3	79.6	199	AZ	11	6.4	113.6	90
FL	29	18.8	53.9	160	OH	18	11.5	40.9	142	AK	3	0.710	571.9	62
DC	3	0.602	0.061	13	WV	5	1.9	24	134	HI	4	1.4	4.2	76
Total	194	113.1	NA	3,149	Total	199	116.4	NA	2,605	Total	135	78.2	NA	1778

AVERAGES FOR THE FIFTY STATES

On average, each state would have eleven electoral votes, 6,174,917 people, cover 70,748 square miles, and have 148 members in the legislature. Currently this would be represented by the states of Arizona, Indiana, Massachusetts, and Tennessee, which have eleven electoral votes each; Missouri, in terms of population (six million); South Dakota, in square mileage (0.814); and Washington, Oklahoma, and Oregon, for members in the legislature (147, 149, and 149, respectively).

NORTH, CENTRAL, AND SOUTH TIER GROUPING

If the states were instead arranged in a North, Central, and South tier grouping, then the averages for each respective grouping would be representative as shown below.

North: AK, ME, WA, ID, MT, ND, MN, WI, MI, OR, NH, VT, NY, SD, MA, CT, and RI.
Averages: 100 electoral votes, 69.2 million population, and 3,690 square miles.

Central: WY, IA, IL, OH, PA, NJ, WV, NE, MO, DC, NV, UT, CO, KS, MD, DE, and IN.
Averages: 155 electoral votes, 86.3 million population, and 2,071 square miles.

South: GA, SC, VA, NC, FL, LA, MS, AL, KY, AR, TN, TX, OK, CA, NM, AZ, and HI.
Averages: 273 electoral votes, 155.6 million population, and 1,771 square miles.

APPENDIX D: FEDERAL TAXES PAID AND RETURNED

At $1	Below $1	Above $1
RI $1	OR 98	GA 1.01
	FL 97	IN 1.05
	TX 94	OH 1.05
	MI 92	PA 1.07
	WA 88	UT 1.07
	WI 86	NC 1.08
	MA 82	VT 1.08
	CO 81	IA 1.10
	NY 79	NE 1.10
	CA 78	WY 1.11
	DE 77	KS 1.12
	IL 75	AZ 1.19
	MN 72	ID 1.21
	NH 71	TN 1.27
	CT 69	MD 1.30
	NV 65	MO 1.32
	NJ 61	SC 1.35
		OK 1.36
		AR 1.41
		ME .10 (of $1.41)
	$3.35	$3.35 Totals

This information of federal tax dollars received per tax dollars paid per state is compiled and consolidated from a Free Republic website and attributed to TaxFoundation.org from 2011. As stated before, what income is used to determine what monies are taken from what sources here as regard to federal benefits is unknown (at least to me). The bottom line is if we are going to equal this out, all the states and DC need to get together and decide what sources to use to determine this. The goal, again if we are to keep this system, is for the states to get their return on $1 for $1. The amounts here, if you want to do the calculation, indicate that, at least for 2011, for every $50 received from the states, $58.54 is paid back to the states.

What the above columns show is that the people in the 17 states Oregon through New Jersey had a shortfall of $3.35 (add the difference between what's showing and $1 and it adds up to $3.35) from the $1 they paid to the federal taxes. The people in the 21 states Georgia through Maine , if effect, received that difference plus the $1 they paid to the federal government. Therefore, if we had just these 38 states, they would account for their $38 total (to include Rhode Island).

This would leave 12 states that received tax money returned to them clearly in excess of the amount of taxes paid, above and beyond the breakeven amount of the first $38. These states (and Maine is counted twice as it was the breakeven state) are follows:

ME 1.31 (remaining of the $1.41)
HI 1.44
MT 1.47
KY 1.51

VA 1.51
SD 1.53
AL 1.66
ND 1.68
WV 1.76
LA 1.78
AK 1.84
MS 2.02
NM 2.03
(DC ?.??)

If we did away with Congress, would most states feel this generous toward other states and go into a fiscal hole if they had to make up the difference?

Basically, from the above figures, of the $50 per person the federal government receives from the 50 states, the federal government "pays" back to the states $58.54. From where, and probably more importantly, from whom, is this extra $8.54 coming from? In addition to other reasons we have such a deficit and debt, this is why members of Congress are called politicians and not accountants.

Those that speak of the bloated, overgrown federal bureaucracy, out of touch federal officials, and over reaching federal government, know that part of the explanation can be attributed to spending beyond its means. If the states were in charge, I seriously doubt they would allow their citizens to be burdened with this accounting system and letting those citizens, along with their children and grandchildren, to assume this financial debt. It would not happen.

www.ingramcontent.com/pod-product-compliance
Lightning Source LLC
Chambersburg PA
CBHW050411290526
45786CB00003B/1220